DAY TRADING FOR BEGINNERS

A Comprehensive Guide to Getting Started

Janie Dolan

INTRODUCTION

Definition Of Day Trading

Day trading refers to the buying and selling of securities within the same trading day. In other words, a day trader purchases a financial instrument such as stocks, currencies, options, or futures, with the intention of selling it within the same trading day. The objective of day trading is to take advantage of the short-term price movements in the market and generate profits from the fluctuations. Day traders typically use technical analysis tools and charts to identify short-term trends and make their trading decisions based on these trends.

Day trading requires a high level of discipline, skill, and knowledge of the financial markets. Day traders must be able to analyze market conditions quickly and accurately, make informed trading decisions, and manage their positions effectively. Day trading is a high-risk activity that requires a significant investment of time and money.

Advantages And Risks Of Day Trading

Day trading offers several advantages and risks that traders should be aware of before engaging in this activity.

Advantages Of Day Trading

1. Quick Profits: Day trading offers the potential for quick profits as traders can take advantage of short-term price movements in the market. Day traders can generate profits from both rising and falling markets by buying low and selling high or selling high and buying low.

2. Independence: Day trading offers traders the opportunity to work independently without the need for a boss or a company. Traders can work from anywhere with an internet connection and have the flexibility to set their own schedule.

3. High Potential Returns: Day trading offers the potential for high returns as traders can leverage their capital to increase their profits. With the right trading strategy, day traders can generate significant profits from a small initial investment.

Risks Of Day Trading

1. High Risk: Day trading is a high-risk activity that requires a significant investment of time and money. Day traders can lose their entire investment if they do not manage their positions effectively.

2. Stressful: Day trading can be a stressful activity as traders need to make quick decisions based on market conditions. The pressure to generate profits quickly can lead to emotional decision making, which can result in losses.

3. Time-Consuming: Day trading requires a significant amount of time and effort as traders need to constantly monitor the market and analyze market conditions. Day traders need to be disciplined and focused to succeed in this activity.

Who Should And Should Not Day Trade

Day trading is not suitable for everyone, and traders should carefully consider their financial situation and risk tolerance before engaging in this activity.

Who Should Day Trade

1. Experienced Traders: Day trading is suitable for experienced traders who have a deep understanding of the financial markets and have a proven track record of successful trading.

2. Risk Takers: Day trading is suitable for risk takers who are willing to take on high-risk investments in exchange for the potential for high returns.

3. Disciplined Traders: Day trading is suitable for disciplined traders who can stick to a trading plan and manage their positions effectively. Successful day traders need to have a high level of discipline and focus to succeed in this activity.

Who Should Not Day Trade

1. Inexperienced Traders: Day trading is not suitable for inexperienced traders who do not have a deep understanding of the financial markets. Inexperienced traders are more likely to make emotional decisions and lose their investment.

2. Risk-Averse Traders: Day trading is not suitable for risk-averse traders who are not willing to take on high-risk investments. Day trading requires a significant investment of time and money and is not suitable for traders who are not comfortable taking on high-risk investments.

3. Impulsive Traders: Day trading is not suitable for impulsive traders who make quick decisions without carefully analyzing market conditions. Impulsive traders are more likely to make emotional decisions and lose their investments.

Importance Of Having A Trading Plan And Risk Management Strategy

One of the key factors that determine the success of a day trader is their ability to plan their trades and manage their risks effectively. A trading plan is a set of rules and guidelines that a trader uses to make their trading decisions. A risk management strategy is a plan that a trader uses to manage their risk exposure and protect their capital. Here are some reasons why having a trading plan and risk management strategy is important for day traders.

Helps to Avoid Emotional Decision Making

A trading plan and risk management strategy help day traders to avoid making emotional decisions. When traders have a plan in place, they are less likely to be influenced by fear or greed, which can lead to irrational decision making. A trading plan and risk management strategy provide a framework for making objective and informed trading decisions.

Improves Consistency

A trading plan and risk management strategy help day traders to be consistent in their trading. When traders have a plan in place, they are more likely to follow a set of rules and guidelines that are based on their trading strategy. This helps to ensure that traders make consistent trading decisions and do not deviate from their strategy.

Minimizes Risk Exposure

A risk management strategy helps day traders to minimize their risk exposure and protect their capital. By setting stop-loss orders and taking profit targets, traders can limit their losses and lock in profits. This helps to ensure that traders do not lose more than they can afford to and can protect their capital from significant losses.

Provides a Framework for Evaluation

A trading plan and risk management strategy provide a framework for evaluating trading performance. Traders can use their trading plan and risk management strategy as a benchmark to measure their success and identify areas for improvement. This helps traders to continuously improve their trading skills and achieve their trading goals.

CHAPTER ONE

Getting Started with Day Trading

Choosing A Broker And Trading Platform

When it comes to trading in the financial markets, choosing the right broker and trading platform is crucial for success. A broker is an intermediary that facilitates buying and selling of financial securities, while a trading platform is a software that allows traders to access markets and execute trades. Here are some factors to consider when choosing a broker and trading platform:

- **Regulation and Reputation**: It is important to choose a regulated broker that operates under the supervision of a reputable financial authority. This ensures that the broker adheres to strict rules and regulations designed to protect investors. Additionally, it is recommended to choose a broker with a good reputation in the industry, with positive reviews and feedback from other traders.

- **Fees and Commissions**: Different brokers charge different fees and commissions for their services. Some brokers charge a flat fee per trade, while others charge a percentage of the trade value. It is important to consider these costs, as they can eat into your profits over time. Additionally, some brokers may offer discounts or promotions for frequent traders.

- **Trading Platform Features**: Different trading platforms offer different features and tools for traders. It is important to choose a platform that meets your needs and preferences. For example, some platforms may offer advanced charting tools, while others may offer social trading features that allow you to follow and copy the trades of other successful traders.

- **Ease of Use and Accessibility**: A good trading platform should be easy to use and accessible from different devices, such as desktop computers, mobile phones, and tablets. Additionally, it should offer fast and reliable execution of trades, with minimal downtime or technical issues.

- **Customer Support**: Finally, it is important to choose a broker that offers good customer support. This includes access to knowledgeable representatives who can help you with any questions or issues you may have, as well as responsive communication channels, such as email, phone, or live chat.

Overall, choosing a broker and trading platform requires careful consideration of multiple factors. It is important to do your research and compare different options before making a decision.

Understanding The Different Types Of Markets And Securities

The financial markets consist of different types of markets and securities, each with its own characteristics and risks. Here are some of the most common types of markets and securities:

- **Stock Market**: The stock market is where shares of publicly traded companies are bought and sold. Stocks represent ownership in a company and can provide returns in the form of dividends and capital gains.

- **Bond Market**: The bond market is where debt securities are bought and sold. Bonds represent loans made to companies or governments and provide returns in the form of interest payments.

- **Forex Market**: The forex market is where currencies are bought and sold. Forex trading involves buying one currency while selling another, with the goal of profiting from changes in exchange rates.

- **Commodity Market**: The commodity market is where physical commodities, such as gold, oil, and agricultural products, are bought and sold. Commodity trading can provide exposure to diverse markets and serve as a hedge against inflation.

- **Futures Market**: The futures market is where contracts to buy or sell commodities or financial assets at a specific price and time in the future are bought and sold. Futures trading involves high leverage and can be risky, but can also provide opportunities for profit.

Overall, understanding the different types of markets and securities is important for diversifying your portfolio and managing risk.

Basic Technical Analysis And Chart Reading

Technical analysis is a method of analyzing financial

markets by examining price and volume data, as well as other indicators, to identify patterns and trends. Here are some basic concepts and techniques used in technical analysis:

- **Trend Analysis**: Trend analysis involves examining charts to identify trends in price movements.

- **Support and Resistance Levels**: Support and resistance levels are price points at which buying or selling pressure is expected to be strong enough to cause a price reversal. Support levels are prices at which demand for a security is expected to be strong enough to prevent further price declines, while resistance levels are prices at which supply of a security is expected to be strong enough to prevent further price increases.

- **Chart Patterns**: Chart patterns are recurring formations on price charts that indicate potential reversals or continuations of trends. Some common chart patterns include head and shoulders, double top/bottom, and triangles.

- **Indicators**: Indicators are mathematical calculations based on price and/or volume data that provide additional insights into market trends and momentum. Examples of indicators include moving averages, relative strength index (RSI), and stochastic oscillators.

While technical analysis can be a useful tool for traders, it is important to keep in mind that it is not a foolproof method and can be subject to interpretation and bias.

Setting Up Your Trading Workstation

Setting up a trading workstation that is optimized for

your trading style and preferences can help improve your trading efficiency and effectiveness. Here are some tips for setting up a trading workstation:

- **Hardware**: A fast and reliable computer with a high-quality monitor(s) is essential for efficient trading. Consider investing in a solid-state drive (SSD) for faster data access, and a backup power supply to prevent data loss in case of power outages.

- **Software**: Choose a trading platform that meets your needs and preferences, and ensure that it is up-to-date and free from bugs and glitches. Additionally, consider using additional software tools such as charting programs and news feeds to supplement your trading analysis.

- **Ergonomics**: Ensure that your trading desk and chair are comfortable and ergonomically designed to prevent discomfort or injury from prolonged use. Additionally, arrange your workspace in a way that minimizes distractions and maximizes focus.

- **Internet Connection**: A fast and stable internet connection is essential for real-time trading. Consider using a wired connection instead of Wi-Fi for faster and more reliable data transfer.

- **Backup and Security**: Ensure that your trading workstation is backed up regularly to prevent data loss in case of hardware failure or other issues. Additionally, ensure that your trading platform and computer are protected by up-to-date antivirus and firewall software, and consider using a virtual private network (VPN) for added security.

Overall, setting up a trading workstation that is optimized for your trading style and preferences can help improve your trading performance and reduce the risk of technical issues or distractions.

CHAPTER TWO

Day Trading Strategies

Scalping

Scalping is a trading strategy that involves buying and selling financial instruments in a short amount of time, usually in seconds or minutes, to make small profits from price fluctuations. Scalpers aim to profit from small price movements by placing a large number of trades. The profits may be small, but the large number of trades executed can generate significant profits over time.

Scalping is a popular trading strategy in the foreign exchange (Forex) market, where traders use leverage to magnify the gains from small price movements. Scalpers use technical indicators and chart patterns to identify short-term trading opportunities. They typically trade in high liquidity markets, such as the major currency pairs, where bid-ask spreads are narrow.

Scalping can be a highly profitable trading strategy, but it requires discipline, patience, and quick reflexes. Scalpers need to be able to enter and exit trades quickly to take advantage of small price movements. They also need to manage their risk carefully, as the profits from each trade are small.

There are several advantages of scalping as a trading strategy. Firstly, it allows traders to profit from small price movements, which can be more predictable than larger movements. Secondly, it can generate consistent profits over time, as long as the trader is disciplined and patient. Finally, scalping can be used in conjunction with other trading strategies, such as swing trading and position trading, to diversify a trader's portfolio.

However, there are also some disadvantages of scalping. Firstly, scalping requires a lot of time and effort, as traders need to monitor the markets constantly and execute trades quickly. Secondly, it can be stressful, as traders need to make split-second decisions and manage their risk carefully. Finally, scalping can be expensive, as traders need to pay commissions and spreads on each trade.

In conclusion, scalping is a trading strategy that involves buying and selling financial instruments in a short amount of time to make small profits from price fluctuations. Scalping can be a highly profitable trading strategy, but it requires discipline, patience, and quick reflexes. Traders who are interested in scalping should carefully consider the advantages and disadvantages of this trading strategy before implementing it in their trading plan.

Momentum Trading

Momentum trading is a trading strategy that involves buying or selling financial instruments based on their recent price movements. Momentum traders believe that stocks that have recently gone up will continue to go up, while stocks that have recently gone down will continue to go down.

Momentum traders use technical analysis to identify stocks that are trending strongly in one direction. They look for stocks that have a high relative strength index (RSI), which is a technical indicator that measures the strength of a stock's price movement. They also look for stocks that are breaking out of a trading range, which is a technical pattern that indicates a shift in market sentiment.

There are several advantages of momentum trading as a trading strategy. Firstly, momentum trading can generate significant profits over a short period of time, as long as the trader can identify strong trends early. Secondly, momentum trading can be used in conjunction with other trading strategies, such as value investing and growth investing, to diversify a trader's portfolio. Finally, momentum trading can be automated using algorithmic trading strategies, which can reduce the amount of time and effort required by the trader.

However, there are also some disadvantages of momentum trading. Firstly, momentum trading can be risky, as stocks that have recently gone up may reverse their trend suddenly. Secondly, momentum trading can be expensive, as traders need to pay commissions and spreads on each trade. Finally, momentum trading can be emotionally taxing, as traders need to manage their risk carefully and avoid making impulsive decisions based on short-term price movements.

In conclusion, momentum trading is a trading strategy that involves buying or selling financial instruments based on their recent price movements. Momentum trading can be a highly profitable trading strategy, but it requires discipline, patience, and a thorough understanding of technical analysis. Traders who are interested in momentum trading should carefully consider the advantages and disadvantages of this trading strategy before implementing it in their trading plan.

Contrarian Trading

Contrarian trading is a trading strategy that involves buying or selling financial instruments that are out of favor with the market. Contrarian traders believe that the market tends to overreact to news and events, leading to temporary price movements that can create buying or selling opportunities.

Contrarian traders use fundamental analysis to identify stocks that are undervalued or overvalued relative to their intrinsic value. They look for stocks that have strong fundamentals, such as a low price-to-earnings ratio, a high dividend yield, or a strong balance sheet. They also look for stocks that are oversold or overbought, based on technical indicators such as the RSI or the stochastic oscillator.

There are several advantages of contrarian trading as a trading strategy. Firstly, contrarian trading can generate significant profits over a long period of time, as long as the trader can identify undervalued or overvalued stocks early. Secondly, contrarian trading can be used in conjunction with other trading strategies, such as value investing and growth investing, to diversify a trader's portfolio. Finally, contrarian trading can be emotionally rewarding, as traders can take advantage of market sentiment and buy or sell stocks that are out of favor with the market.

However, there are also some disadvantages of contrarian trading. Firstly, contrarian trading can be risky, as stocks that are out of favor with the market may continue to decline or fail to recover. Secondly, contrarian trading can be expensive, as traders need to pay commissions and spreads on each trade. Finally, contrarian trading can be emotionally challenging, as traders need to have the patience and discipline to wait for the market to recognize the value of their chosen stocks.

In conclusion, contrarian trading is a trading strategy that involves buying or selling financial instruments that are out of favor with the market. Contrarian trading can be a highly profitable trading strategy, but it requires discipline, patience, and a thorough understanding of fundamental and technical analysis. Traders who are interested in contrarian trading should carefully consider the advantages and disadvantages of this trading strategy before implementing it in their trading plan.

Breakout Trading

Breakout trading is a trading strategy that involves buying or selling financial instruments when they break through a support or resistance level. Breakout traders believe that when a stock breaks through a significant price level, it is a sign that a new trend is starting and that it is a good time to buy or sell the stock.

Breakout traders use technical analysis to identify stocks that are breaking through significant price levels. They look for stocks that are breaking through a trading range, a trendline, or a moving average. They also look for stocks that have high trading volume, which can confirm the strength of the breakout.

There are several advantages of breakout trading as a

trading strategy. Firstly, breakout trading can generate significant profits over a short period of time, as long as the trader can identify strong breakouts early. Secondly, breakout trading can be used in conjunction with other trading strategies, such as trend following and momentum trading, to diversify a trader's portfolio. Finally, breakout trading can be automated using algorithmic trading strategies, which can reduce the amount of time and effort required by the trader.

However, there are also some disadvantages of breakout trading. Firstly, breakout trading can be risky, as stocks that break out may reverse their trend suddenly. Secondly, breakout trading can be expensive, as traders need to pay commissions and spreads on each trade. Finally, breakout trading can be emotionally challenging,mas traders need to have the discipline to cut losses and take profits at the right time.

In conclusion, breakout trading is a trading strategy that involves buying or selling financial instruments when they break through a significant price level. Breakout trading can be a highly profitable trading strategy, but it requires discipline, patience, and a thorough understanding of technical analysis. Traders who are interested in breakout trading should carefully consider the advantages and disadvantages of this trading strategy before implementing it in their trading plan.

News-Based Trading

News-based trading is a trading strategy that involves buying or selling financial instruments based on news and events that affect the market. News-based traders believe that news and events can significantly affect the prices of financial instruments, and that it is important to be aware of these news and events to make profitable trades.

News-based traders use fundamental analysis to identify news and events that may affect the market. They look for news and events that are likely to have a significant impact on the economy or the financial sector, such as interest rate decisions, earnings reports, and geopolitical events. They also look for news and events that are likely to affect specific companies or industries, such as mergers and acquisitions, regulatory changes, and technological breakthroughs.

There are several advantages of news-based trading as a trading strategy. Firstly, news-based trading can generate significant profits over a short period of time, as long as the trader can identify important news and events early. Secondly, news-based trading can be used in conjunction with other trading strategies, such as trend following and breakout trading, to diversify a trader's portfolio. Finally, news-based trading can be automated using algorithmic trading strategies, which can reduce the amount of time and effort required by the trader.

However, there are also some disadvantages of news-based trading. Firstly, news-based trading can be risky, as news and events can be unpredictable and their impact on the market may be short-lived. Secondly, news-based trading can be expensive, as traders need to pay commissions and spreads on each trade. Finally, news-based trading can be emotionally challenging, as traders need to have the discipline to cut losses and take profits at the right time.

In conclusion, news-based trading is a trading strategy that involves buying or selling financial instruments based on news and events that affect the market. News-based trading can be a highly profitable trading strategy, but it requires discipline, patience, and a thorough understanding of fundamental analysis. Traders who are interested in news-based trading should carefully consider the advantages and disadvantages of this trading strategy before implementing it in their trading plan.

CHAPTER FOUR

Risk Management Techniques

Setting Stop-Loss Orders

Setting stop-loss orders is an essential risk management technique used by traders and investors to limit their losses in case the market moves against their positions. A stop-loss order is an instruction to automatically sell or buy a security once its price reaches a specific level, known as the stop price. By setting a stop-loss order, traders can prevent their losses from exceeding a certain amount and protect their capital from catastrophic losses.

Types of Stop-Loss Orders

There are two main types of stop-loss orders that traders can use: the traditional stop-loss order and the trailing stop-loss order. A traditional stop-loss order is a fixed order that stays in place until the security reaches the stop price. Once the stop price is reached, the order becomes a market order, and the security is sold or bought at the prevailing market price. In contrast, a trailing stop-loss order is a dynamic order that adjusts the stop price based on the price movements of the security. The stop price is set a certain distance away from the current market price, and as the security moves in favor of the trade, the stop price moves along with it. This allows traders to lock in profits while also limiting their losses.

Setting Stop-Loss Orders

To set a stop-loss order, traders need to determine their risk tolerance and the appropriate stop price. The stop price should be set at a level that allows for a reasonable amount of price volatility while also limiting the potential loss. Traders should also consider the market conditions and the trading strategy being used when setting the stop-loss order.

Benefits of Setting Stop-Loss Orders

Setting stop-loss orders has several benefits for traders. Firstly, it helps to reduce emotional trading decisions by taking the decision-making process out of the hands of the trader. Secondly, it helps to limit losses and protect capital from catastrophic losses. Finally, it allows traders to focus on their trading strategies and not on constantly monitoring the markets.

Using Trailing Stops

Using trailing stops is an effective way for traders to protect their profits while also limiting their losses. A trailing stop is a dynamic order that adjusts the stop price based on the price movements of the security. As the security moves in favor of the trade, the stop price moves along with it, allowing traders to lock in profits while also limiting their losses.

Advantages of Trailing Stops

One of the main advantages of using trailing stops is that it allows traders to lock in profits. As the security moves in favor of the trade, the stop price is adjusted upwards, allowing traders to capture a greater portion of the profit. Additionally, trailing stops can help to protect profits from market reversals, ensuring that profits are not given back to the market. Finally, trailing stops can help to limit losses by allowing traders to exit a losing trade once the stop price is reached.

Disadvantages of Trailing Stops

While there are many advantages to using trailing stops, there are also some disadvantages that traders need to be aware of. Firstly, trailing stops can be more complex than traditional stop-loss orders, requiring more skill and experience to use effectively. Secondly, trailing stops can be more sensitive to market volatility, causing them to trigger prematurely in volatile markets. Finally, trailing stops can lead to missed opportunities for profit, as they may cause traders to exit a trade too early.

Managing Position Sizing

Managing position sizing is a critical component of successful trading. Position sizing refers to the amount of capital that a trader allocates to each trade. By managing position sizing, traders can ensure that they are using their capital efficiently and effectively, while also minimizing their risk exposure.

Factors to Consider when Managing Position Sizing

When managing position sizing, traders need to consider several factors. Firstly, they need to consider their risk tolerance and the amount of capital they apportion to each trade. Traders should never risk more than they can afford to lose on any single trade. Secondly, traders need to consider the market conditions and the volatility of the security they are trading. Higher volatility securities require smaller position sizes to limit risk exposure. Finally, traders need to consider their trading strategy and the potential returns of the trade when determining position size.

Benefits of Managing Position Sizing

Managing position sizing has several benefits for traders. Firstly, it helps to minimize risk exposure, limiting the potential losses on any single trade. Secondly, it helps traders to use their capital more efficiently, ensuring that they are not tying up too much capital on any one trade. Finally, it allows traders to diversify their portfolio, making it easier to manage risk across multiple trades.

Avoiding Overtrading And Revenge Trading

Overtrading and revenge trading are two common mistakes that traders make that can lead to significant losses. Overtrading refers to the act of trading too frequently, often resulting in lower quality trades and higher transaction costs. Revenge trading refers to the act of making impulsive trades in an attempt to recoup losses from previous trades. Both of these behaviors can be detrimental to a trader's success.

Signs of Overtrading

There are several signs that a trader may be overtrading. Firstly, they may be making too many trades in a short period of time, often resulting in lower quality trades. Secondly, they may be taking on too much risk, allocating too much capital to each trade. Finally, they may be experiencing high transaction costs, as frequent trading often results in higher fees and commissions.

How To Avoid Overtrading

To avoid overtrading, traders should focus on quality over quantity. They should only enter trades that meet their criteria, and they should avoid making impulsive trades based on emotions or market noise. Traders should also set realistic goals and limits for their trading activities, including daily and weekly trade limits and profit targets.

Signs of Revenge Trading

Revenge trading is often characterized by impulsive and emotional trades. Traders may enter trades without proper analysis or without following their trading plan. Revenge trading is often triggered by a significant loss or a series of losses, leading traders to make impulsive trades in an attempt to recoup their losses.

How to Avoid Revenge Trading

To avoid revenge trading, traders should focus on maintaining emotional discipline and sticking to their trading plan. Traders should take breaks and step away from the markets if they feel emotionally overwhelmed. Additionally, traders should have a plan in place for dealing with losses, including stop-loss orders and a clear understanding of their risk tolerance. Finally, traders should focus on their long-term trading goals, rather than attempting to recoup losses in the short-term.

CHAPTER FIVE

Advanced Trading Techniques

Using Leverage And Margin

Leverage and margin are two concepts that are widely used in financial markets. They allow traders and investors to amplify their potential returns by using borrowed funds. Leverage is the use of borrowed money to increase the size of a trade or investment, while margin is the amount of money that is required to be held in an account in order to use leverage.

One of the most common ways to use leverage is through margin trading, which is available in many financial markets such as stocks, forex, and cryptocurrencies. With margin trading, traders are able to borrow funds from their brokers to increase their trading capital. This means that they can make larger trades than they would be able to with their own capital alone.

However, leverage also magnifies losses, which means that traders can lose more than their initial investment. Therefore, it is important for traders to manage their risk carefully when using leverage. Traders should also ensure that they have sufficient margin in their accounts to cover their positions, as failure to do so could result in forced liquidation of their trades.

In addition to margin trading, leverage can also be used in other ways such as through the use of derivatives like futures and options. With futures, traders can use leverage to amplify their exposure to an underlying asset without actually owning it. Options also offer traders the ability to use leverage, as the premium paid for an option is typically much less than the cost of owning the underlying asset.

Overall, leverage and margin can be powerful tools for traders and investors to increase their potential returns, but they should be used carefully and with a thorough understanding of the risks involved.

Short Selling

Short selling is a strategy used by traders to profit from a decline in the price of an asset. This is done by borrowing the asset from a broker and selling it in the market with the expectation that the price will fall. If the price does fall, the trader can buy back the asset at a lower price, return it to the broker, and pocket the difference as profit.

Short selling can be a risky strategy, as losses can be unlimited if the price of the asset rises instead of falling. This is because the trader is obligated to buy back the asset at the market price in order to return it to the broker, regardless of how high the price goes.

Short selling is also subject to certain rules and regulations in many markets. For example, some markets require that the trader have a certain amount of margin in their account to cover any potential losses, while others may have restrictions on when and how short selling can be done.

Despite these risks and regulations, short selling can be a useful strategy for traders who are able to identify assets that are overvalued or likely to decline in price. Short selling can also be used to hedge against long positions in the same asset, as it can provide a way to profit from a decline in price while still holding a long position.

Trading Options

Options are a type of derivative that give traders the right, but not the obligation, to buy or sell an underlying asset at a certain price and time. Trading options can be a complex strategy, but it can also offer traders the ability to profit from a range of market conditions.

One of the key advantages of trading options is the ability to use leverage. This means that traders can control a large amount of underlying asset with a relatively small investment. Options also offer a wide range of strategies, including the ability to profit from both bullish and bearish market conditions.

However, trading options can also be risky, as losses can be significant if the market moves against the trader. It is important for traders to have a thorough understanding of the risks involved in trading options, as well as the different strategies that are available.

Options trading also requires a certain level of knowledge and experience, as well as access to advanced tools and platforms. Traders need to understand the different types of options, including call and put options, as well as the factors that affect their prices such as implied volatility and time decay.

One popular options trading strategy is the covered call, which involves owning the underlying asset and selling a call option on that asset. This allows traders to generate income from the premium received for selling the call option, while also potentially benefiting from a rise in the price of the underlying asset.

Another popular options trading strategy is the straddle, which involves buying both a call option and a put option on the same underlying asset at the same strike price and expiration date. This allows traders to profit from a large price movement in either direction, while limiting their potential losses to the premium paid for the options.

Overall, options trading can be a powerful tool for traders looking to diversify their portfolio and profit from a range of market conditions. However, it is important to have a solid understanding of the risks and complexities involved in options trading before getting started.

Understanding Market Depth And Level 2 Data

Market depth and level 2 data are two important concepts for traders looking to gain a deeper understanding of the market and make more informed trading decisions. Market depth refers to the level of supply and demand for an asset at different price levels, while level 2 data provides a detailed view of the current bid and ask prices for an asset.

Market depth can be visualized using a market depth chart, which displays the number of buy and sell orders at different price levels. This can help traders to identify areas of support and resistance for an asset, as well as potential price levels where there may be a large number of buyers or sellers.

Level 2 data provides even more detail, as it displays the current bid and ask prices for an asset, as well as the number of shares or contracts available at each price level. This allows traders to see the current supply and demand for an asset in real-time, and can help them to identify potential buying or selling opportunities.

Level 2 data is typically only available to professional traders or those with advanced trading platforms. However, some brokers may offer limited access to level 2 data for retail traders.

Overall, market depth and level 2 data can be powerful tools for traders looking to gain a deeper understanding of the market and make more informed trading decisions. However, it is important to have a solid understanding of these concepts and how to use them effectively before incorporating them into a trading strategy.

CHAPTER SIX

Psychology of Day Trading

Common Biases And Cognitive Errors

Biases and cognitive errors are common mental shortcuts that people use to make decisions and judgments. These shortcuts can be useful in certain situations, but they can also lead to errors in judgment and decision-making. There are many different biases and cognitive errors, but some of the most common ones are:

- Confirmation Bias: The tendency to search for, interpret, and remember information in a way that confirms one's preexisting beliefs or hypotheses. This can lead to overconfidence and errors in judgment.

- Availability Heuristic: The tendency to judge the likelihood of an event based on how easily examples come to mind. This can lead to overestimating the likelihood of rare events and underestimating the likelihood of common events.

- Anchoring Bias: The tendency to rely too heavily on the first piece of information encountered when making decisions. This can lead to errors in judgment and decision-making.

- Hindsight Bias: The tendency to believe, after

an event has occurred, that one would have predicted or expected the outcome. This can lead to overconfidence and errors in judgment.

- Overconfidence Bias: The tendency to overestimate one's abilities or the accuracy of one's beliefs and predictions. This can lead to overconfidence and errors in judgment.

It is important to be aware of these biases and cognitive errors, as they can have a significant impact on our decision-making and judgment. By recognizing these biases, we can try to overcome them and make more accurate and rational decisions.

Keeping Emotions In Check

Emotions can play a powerful role in our decision-making and behavior. While emotions can be helpful in certain situations, they can also lead to impulsive or irrational decisions. To keep emotions in check, it is important to:

- Recognize and identify emotions: One of the first steps to keeping emotions in check is to recognize and identify them. By being aware of our emotions, we can better understand how they may be influencing our decision-making.

- Take a step back: When emotions are running high, it can be helpful to take a step back and give ourselves some space. This can help us to think more clearly and rationally.

- Practice mindfulness: Mindfulness can be a helpful tool for managing emotions. By focusing on the present moment and observing our thoughts and feelings without judgment, we can develop greater awareness and control over our emotions.

- Seek support: It can be helpful to seek support from others when dealing with difficult emotions. This can include talking to friends or family members, seeking professional counseling, or joining a support group.

By keeping emotions in check, we can make more rational and effective decisions and avoid making impulsive or harmful choices.

Dealing With Losses And Setbacks

Losses and setbacks are a natural part of life, but they can be difficult to deal with. To effectively cope with losses and setbacks, it is important to:

- Allow time to grieve: It is important to allow ourselves time to grieve and process the loss or setback. This may involve expressing our feelings, seeking support from others, or engaging in activities that help us to relax and reduce stress.

- Reframe the situation: While it may be difficult to see at the time, setbacks and losses can provide opportunities for growth and learning. By reframing the situation in a positive light and focusing on what we can learn from it, we can develop resilience and move forward.

- Practice self-care: Taking care of ourselves is important when dealing with losses and setbacks. This may involve engaging in activities that promote physical and emotional well-being, such as exercise, meditation, or spending time with loved ones.

- Seek support: It can be helpful to seek support from others when dealing with losses and setbacks. This can include talking to friends or family members, seeking professional counseling, or joining a support group. By sharing our experiences with others, we can gain new perspectives and find comfort and understanding.

- Set realistic goals: When dealing with a loss or setback, it is important to set realistic goals for ourselves. This can help us to focus on what is within our control and avoid becoming overwhelmed by the situation.

- Practice gratitude: Practicing gratitude can help us to shift our focus from what we have lost to what we still have. By focusing on the positive aspects of our lives, we can develop greater resilience and cope more effectively with losses and setbacks.

By taking these steps, we can effectively cope with losses and setbacks and develop greater resilience in the face of adversity.

Maintaining Discipline And Consistency

Maintaining discipline and consistency is essential for achieving our goals and making meaningful progress in our lives. To maintain discipline and consistency, it is important to:

- Set clear goals: Clear and specific goals can help us to stay focused and motivated. By setting goals that are meaningful and achievable, we can develop a sense of purpose and direction.

- Develop a plan: A clear plan of action can help us to stay on track and make progress towards our goals. This may involve breaking larger goals into smaller, more manageable steps, and establishing a regular routine.

- Hold ourselves accountable: Holding ourselves

accountable can help us to stay motivated and on track. This may involve tracking our progress, setting deadlines, or seeking support from others.

- Practice self-discipline: Self-discipline involves making conscious choices and taking actions that are aligned with our goals and values. This may involve developing healthy habits, avoiding distractions, and managing our time effectively.

- Practice self-compassion: While discipline and consistency are important, it is also important to practice self-compassion. This may involve being kind to ourselves when we make mistakes, recognizing our progress and accomplishments, and taking time to rest and recharge.

By maintaining discipline and consistency, we can achieve our goals and make meaningful progress in our lives. By taking a deliberate and intentional approach to our actions, we can build habits and behaviors that support our growth and well-being.

CHAPTER SEVEN

Best Practices and Resources

Tracking Your Trades And Performance

As a day trader, tracking your trades and performance is essential to becoming a successful trader. Keeping track of your trades will help you understand your strengths and weaknesses, as well as your successes and failures. This information will help you make better trading decisions in the future.

One of the best ways to track your trades is to keep a trading journal. A trading journal is a record of all your trades, including the date, time, entry and exit prices, position size, and any other relevant information. By recording this information, you can analyze your trades and identify patterns and trends.

In addition to keeping a trading journal, it's also important to track your performance metrics. Performance metrics can help you measure your progress as a trader and identify areas for improvement. Some common performance metrics include win rate, average profit/loss per trade, and maximum drawdown. By tracking these metrics over time, you can identify trends in your performance and make adjustments to your trading strategy accordingly.

Reviewing And Analyzing Your Trading Data

Once you've started tracking your trades and performance, the next step is to review and analyze your trading data. This process can help you identify patterns and trends in your trading behavior, as well as areas for improvement.

One of the most effective ways to analyze your trading data is to use a spreadsheet or trading software that can help you visualize your data. You can use these tools to create charts and graphs that show your performance metrics over time, as well as your trading history and positions.

When analyzing your trading data, it's important to be objective and honest with yourself. Don't be afraid to identify your weaknesses and areas for improvement. This information can help you develop a better trading strategy and ultimately become a more successful trader.

Learning From Experienced Traders And Mentors

Learning from experienced traders and mentors is a great way to improve your trading skills and become a more successful trader. Experienced traders can offer valuable insights and advice based on their own experiences in the market.

One way to connect with experienced traders is to join a trading community or forum. These communities are a great place to ask questions, share ideas, and learn from other traders. You can also consider finding a mentor who can provide one-on-one guidance and support.

JANIE DOLAN

CONCLUSION

Recap of key takeaways and lessons learned

Day trading is a popular trading strategy that involves buying and selling securities within the same trading day. It requires a great deal of knowledge, skill, and discipline to be successful. Here are some key takeaways and lessons learned that can help you become a successful day trader.

Understand the Markets

Before you start day trading, it is important to have a deep understanding of the markets. This includes understanding how different markets work, the factors that affect prices, and how to read charts and other technical indicators. This knowledge will help you make informed trading decisions and minimize the risks involved.

Develop a Trading Plan

One of the keys to success in day trading is to have a well-defined trading plan. Your plan should include your trading goals, the types of securities you will trade, the strategies you will use, and the risk management techniques you will employ. A good trading plan will help you stay focused and disciplined, and avoid making emotional and impulsive trading decisions.

Manage Your Risks

Day trading involves a high level of risk, and it is important to manage your risks effectively. This includes setting stop-loss orders to limit your losses, avoiding trading with too much leverage, and diversifying your portfolio to spread your risks. You should also be prepared for unexpected events, such as market volatility and news releases, which can have a significant impact on prices.

Stay Disciplined

Discipline is a critical factor in day trading. You should stick to your trading plan and avoid making emotional and impulsive decisions. This includes avoiding the temptation to chase profits or to try to recoup losses by taking excessive risks. You should also have a strict risk management plan and be prepared to exit trades that are not performing as expected.

Learn from Your Mistakes

Day trading is a learning process, and you will make mistakes along the way. It is important to learn from these mistakes and use them to improve your trading strategy. This includes keeping a trading journal to record your trades and analyze your performance, as well as seeking feedback from other traders and experts in the field.

Stay Informed

To be successful in day trading, you need to stay informed about market trends and news that can affect prices. This includes following economic indicators, company earnings reports, and political developments. You should also stay up-to-date on changes in regulations and trading rules that can impact your trading strategy.

Final Tips for Success in Day Trading

Day trading can be a challenging but rewarding activity. Here are some final tips to help you achieve success in day trading.

Start Small

When you first start day trading, it is important to start small and build up your experience and confidence. This means trading with a small amount of capital and gradually increasing your position sizes as you become more comfortable with the markets and your trading strategy.

Stick to Liquid Securities

Liquid securities, such as stocks and exchange-traded funds (ETFs), are easier to trade and provide more opportunities for liquidity and price movement. They also tend to have tighter bid-ask spreads, which can reduce your trading costs and increase your profitability.

Use a Reliable Trading Platform

Choosing a reliable trading platform is critical for day trading success. Your trading platform should be fast, secure, and provide access to real-time market data and trading tools. It should also have a user-friendly interface and reliable customer support.

Stay Focused and Disciplined

Day trading requires a great deal of focus and discipline. You should avoid distractions and stay focused on your trading plan and strategy. This includes avoiding social media and other non-trading-related activities during trading hours. You should also stay disciplined and avoid making emotional and impulsive trading decisions.

Manage Your Emotions

Managing your emotions is critical for day trading success. You should avoid becoming too attached to your positions, and avoid trading based on fear, greed, or other emotions. This can lead to making irrational trading decisions and losses. One way to manage your emotions is to use a trading plan and stick to it. This can help you avoid making impulsive decisions and stay focused on your long-term goals.

Continuously Learn and Improve

The markets are constantly changing, and it is important to continuously learn and improve your trading strategy. This includes keeping up-to-date with news and events that can impact the markets, as well as seeking out education and training opportunities. You can also learn from other traders and experts in the field, and use this knowledge to refine your trading strategy and improve your performance.

Be Prepared for the Unexpected

Day trading involves a high level of risk, and unexpected events can occur at any time. It is important to be prepared for these events and have a plan in place to manage them. This includes setting stop-loss orders to limit your losses, having a backup plan in case of technical issues or other problems, and being prepared for market volatility and news releases that can have a significant impact on prices.

Take Breaks and Manage Your Health

Day trading can be a stressful and demanding activity, and it is important to take breaks and manage your health. This includes taking regular breaks to rest your mind and recharge your batteries, as well as maintaining a healthy diet and exercise routine. You should also manage your stress levels and avoid burnout by taking time off when needed.

Stay Positive and Persistent

Finally, staying positive and persistent is critical for day trading success. You will face challenges and setbacks along the way, but it is important to stay focused on your goals and believe in your abilities. You should also stay persistent and not give up easily, even when facing losses or other difficulties. By staying positive and persistent, you can overcome obstacles and achieve success in day trading.

In conclusion, day trading can be a rewarding but challenging activity that requires a great deal of knowledge, skill, and discipline. By understanding the markets, developing a trading plan, managing your risks, staying disciplined, learning from your mistakes, and following these final tips, you can increase your chances of success in day trading. Remember to start small, stick to liquid securities, use a reliable trading platform, manage your emotions, continuously learn and improve, be prepared for the unexpected, take breaks and manage your health, and stay positive and persistent. With these strategies in place, you can become a successful day trader and achieve your financial goals.

www.ingramcontent.com/pod-product-compliance
Lightning Source LLC
Chambersburg PA
CBHW070801220526
45467CB00017B/739